So Glad We're Friends

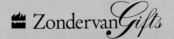Zondervan*Gifts*

Acknowledgments:

Some quotations for this book were taken from the following:
Eleanor Doan, THE COMPLETE SPEAKERS SOURCEBOOK, Zondervan Publishing House, 1996;
   p. 8, 11, 20, 22, 32, 41.
Robert I. Fitzhenry, ed., THE HARPER BOOK OF QUOTATIONS, 3rd ed., HarperPerennial, a division of
   HarperCollins Publishers, 1993; p. 18, 23.
Frank S. Mead, ed., 12,000 RELIGIOUS QUOTATIONS, Baker Book House, 1989; p. 2, 14, 16, 25.
James Dalton Morrison, ed., MASTERPIECES OF RELIGIOUS VERSE, Baker Book House, 1977;
   p. 14, 23, 30, 36.
George Sweeting, WHO SAID THAT?, Moody Press, 1995; p. 7, 39, 41, 42.
R.E.O. White, YOU CAN SAY THAT AGAIN, Zondervan Publishing House, 1991; p. 10, 12, 14, 20, 26, 29, 44.

Copyright Information:

So Glad We're Friends
Copyright © 1997 by The Zondervan Corporation
ISBN 0-310-97059-8

Requests for information should be addressed to: ☷ ZondervanPublishingHouse
                                                    Grand Rapids, Michigan 49530

                                                    http://www.zondervan.com

Senior Editor: Joy Marple
Project Editor: Sarah Hupp
Illustration: Yolanda Gonzalez

Printed in China

To: _____

May God make your days joyful ones... for you are a joy to me.

From: _____

The Miracle of Friendship

There's a miracle called friendship
That dwells within the heart,
And you don't know how it happens
Or when it gets its start.
But the happiness it brings you
Always gives a special lift,
And you realize that friendship
Is life's most precious gift.

A good friend is like a wonderful book ...
The inside is even better than the cover!

Anonymous

I thank my God every time I remember you.

Philippians 1:3

My friend is one who speaks to me

and takes the time to write;

Who has a thought to spare for me

whatever day or night;

The one who knows the faults I have,

but does not criticize,

And who is always at my side

to help and sympathize.

My friend is one who keeps me in

her constant memory,

And now and then will turn to God

and say a prayer for me.

after Don Dupuy

Love each other deeply...

1 Peter 4:8a

A true friend is the gift of God, and he only who made hearts can unite them.

Robert South

Of all the lovely treasures
At the rainbow's brilliant end,
One brings lasting pleasure:
A dear and trusted friend.

Anonymous

Your love has given me
great joy and encouragement

Philemon 7

Lord, help my friend to glimpse the rainbow through the tears, to see your light shining in the darkest night, and to behold your love reflected in me. Amen.

My Friend

Who always shares a sunny smile?

Sits and visits for a while?

Walks with me that extra mile?

My friend does.

Who lets me know I'm understood?

Never speaks a word that's rude?

Does things helpful, kind and good?

My friend does.

Who's this friend who cares for me?

Helps and comforts willingly?

Mirrors Christ in all I see?

Y–O–U–!

Sarah Michaels

May the God of hope fill you with
all joy and peace as you trust in him.

Romans 15:13a

Those who bring sunshine into
the lives of others, cannot keep it
from themselves.

James M. Barrie

Sweet is the Journey

Friendship is a chain of gold

Shaped in God's all perfect mold.

Each link a smile, a laugh, a tear,

A grip of the hand, a word of cheer.

Steadfast as the ages roll

Binding closer soul to soul;

No matter how far or heavy the load

Sweet is the journey on friendship's road.

Author Unknown

A true friend shares freely,
advises justly, assists readily, adventures boldly,
takes all patiently, defends courageously,
and continues a friend unchangeably.

William Penn

There is a friend
who sticks closer than a brother.

Proverbs 18:24b

Oh, the comfort, the inexpressible comfort

of feeling safe with a person,

having neither to weigh thoughts,

nor measure words,

but pouring them all right out — just as they are,

chaff and grain together —

certain that a faithful hand

will take and sift them...

keep what is worth keeping...

and with the breath of kindness

blow the rest away.

Dinah Maria Mulock Craik

You have filled my heart
with greater joy.

Psalm 4:7a

Life has no blessing like a caring friend.

A Friend Like You

When it's cloudy outside

I have sun in my day

Because of a friend like you.

When my purse holds no coin

I'm still richer than kings

Because of a friend like you.

Friends like you share the good times.

Friends like you share the tough times;

And all in—between times too.

And though I don't say it

As oft' as I should

I'm glad for a friend like you.

Sarah Michaels

Perfume and incense bring joy
to the heart, and the pleasantness
of one's friend springs from his
earnest counsel.

Proverbs 27:9

It brings comfort to have friends
in whatever happens.

Saint John Chrysostom

Did you know you were brave,

did you know you were strong?

Did you know there was one leaning hard?

Did you know that I waited

and listened and prayed,

And was cheered by your simplest word?

Did you know that I longed

for that smile on your face,

For the sound of your voice ringing true?

Did you know I grew stronger and better

because I have merely been friends with you?

Two are better than one,
because they have a good return for their work:
if one falls down, his friend can help him up.

Ecclesiastes 4:9-10a

Good friends are like
the evening shadows:
they increase in importance
until the sun of life sets.

after Johann Gottfried von Herder

Every day I pray for God to bless you as you
have blessed me, my friend. And I thank him for
your gift of friendship's shared joys and sorrows. You
are in my heart, my thoughts, my prayers...you are
my friend.

A friend is a present you give to yourself!

A new command I give you:
Love one another.
As I have loved you,
so you must love one another.

John 13:34

A Comforting Thought

There's a comforting thought at the close of the day,
When I'm weary and lonely and sad,
That sort of grips hold of my crusty old heart
And bids it be merry and glad.
It gets in my soul and drives out the blues,
And finally thrills through and through.
It is just a sweet memory that chants the refrain:
"I'm glad for good friends just like you!"

Author Unknown

The Lord bless you and keep you;
the Lord make his face shine upon
you and be gracious to you; the
Lord turn his face toward you and
give you peace.

Numbers 6:24-26

A Prayer

I ask not ownership of vast estates

Nor piles of gold —

But make me generous with the little store

My hands now hold.

Nor shall I ask that life should give to me

Another friend —

Just keep me true to those I have, dear Lord,

Until the end.

B.Y. Williams

Be devoted to one another in brotherly love.

Romans 12:10

[God] chooses our relatives,

we choose our friends.

Jacques Delille

i'm thankful i chose you.

You always let me blow off steam

And don't condemn me for it.

And when I've made a huge mistake

You kindly will ignore it.

You let me be just who I am

Right now, this very day.

God bless you, my special friend.

I'm glad you came my way.

Conover

May the Lord show kindness to you,

as you have shown...to me.

Ruth 1:8

Laughter.

The joy of sharing

the same sense of humor.

Knowledge.

Separate and shared.

Yours, mine, ours.

Support.

Always there when needed

to back each other up.

Friendship.

One of God's best gifts.

Conover

May he give you the desire of your heart
and make all your plans succeed.

Psalm 20:4

The Best Treasure

There are veins in the hills where jewels hide,

And gold lies buried deep;

There are harbor-towns where the great ships ride,

And fame and fortune sleep;

But land and sea though we tireless rove,

And follow each trail to the end,

Whatever the wealth of our treasure-trove,

The best we shall find is a friend.

John J. Moment

You, my friend, are the rainbow of my life:
the pastel, the bright;
the pot of gold;
the promise after the storm;
the reminder that God loves me.

Conover

It is right for me to feel this way about...you,
since I have you in my heart.

Philippians 1:7

Little Things

It's just the little, homely things,

The unobtrusive, friendly things,

The "Won't-you-let-me-help-you" things

That make the pathway light.

The "Done-and-then-forgotten" things,....

The "Laugh-with-me-it's-funny" things,

The "Never-mind-the-trouble" things,

That make our world seem bright.

For all the countless, famous things,....

Can't match the little, human things,

Those "Oh-it's-simply-nothing" things,

That make us happy, quite.

Eva M. Hinckley

Friendship is one of the sweetest
joys of life. Many might have failed
beneath the bitterness of their trial
had they not found a friend.

Charles Haddon Spurgeon

[Jesus said,] "You are my friends
if you do what I command."

John 15:14

A friend is someone who shares with you
a smile, a tear, a hand.
A friend is someone who cares for you;
a heart that understands.
A friend is someone you can be with
when there's nothing to do.
A friend is someone you can laugh with —
I'm so glad that friend is you.

Conover

Dear friends, let us love one another,
for love comes from God.

1 John 4:7

I'm thankful for your cheerful words;

Appreciate your smile;

I'm pleased you are considerate —

No one would you revile.

I'm grateful for your humor,

And your humility;

But most of all I'm thankful that

You've been a friend to me.

Sarah Michaels

Greater love has no one than this,
that he lay down his life for his friends.

John 15:13

Old Friends

Friendships that have stood the test —
Time and change — are surely best;
Brow may wrinkle, hair grow gray,
Friendship never knows decay.
Cherish friendship in your breast —
New is good, but old is best;
Make new friends, but keep the old;
Those are silver, these are gold.

Joseph Parry

He who clasps the hand of a friend
holds tight to a blessing.

Dear friend, I pray...
that all may go well with you.

3 John 2

It is my joy in life to find

At every turning of the road

The strong arms of a friend who's kind

To help me onward with my load.

And since I have no gold to give

And love alone can make amends,

My only prayer is, "While I live,

God, make me worthy of my friends!"

Author Unknown

Thank You, Friend

I know I've never told you

In the hurried rush of days

How much your friendship helps me

In a thousand little ways;

But you've played such a part

In all I do or try to be,

I want to tell you thank you

For being friends with me.

Author Unknown

Two is such a cozy number

most especially

when one of those two is you

and the other one is me.

God always knew

that together our one and one

would make the perfect two.

Two hearts that feel each other's pain.

Two souls that share a faith.

Two minds that help each other grow.

I'm so glad God sent you

to make my perfect two.

Conover

A friend loves at all times.

Proverbs 17 : 17

The Best Treasure

There's happiness in little things,
There's joy in passing pleasure.
But friendships are, from year to year,
The best of all life's treasure.